WHISPERS OF THE SOUL: AWAKENED BY LOVE

Poetry

by Olga Tomaszewski

WHISPERS OF THE SOUL: AWAKENED BY LOVE

Poetry

by Olga Tomaszewski

Table Of Contents

When Your Heart Opens Love is Endless

The Echo
I did not seek you,
yet you found me in the quiet places,
where whispers of longing
had long been silenced.

You were a stranger,
yet your voice felt like a melody
I had forgotten,
a song from another life,
another time.

In your eyes,
I caught a glimpse of the self
I was meant to be—
unbound, whole, luminous.

And though I cannot reach for you,
your presence lingers,
an echo that stirs my soul awake.
You are the whisper,
the ache.
the beginning of a love
I now give to myself.

Soul's Embrace
There was a moment,
a breath,
when I realized I was not lost,
but waiting to be found.

In the quiet of my own heart,
I had forgotten
that love could be more
than a longing unspoken,
more than a dream untold.

And you,
you came to me
not with words,
but with a presence
that felt like home—
a place my soul had always known.

You are not a man to me,
but a mirror,
reflecting back the parts of myself
I had long neglected,
the pieces I left behind
in the shadow of my fears.

Now,
I stand before you,
whole—
not because of what you've given,
but because of what you've awakened
within me.

I no longer seek,
for I have found.
And though our paths may never fully cross,
your love has touched me,
and I am forever changed

Silent Knowing
In the quiet moments
between breaths,
I feel you near—
not with my eyes,
but with something deeper,
a knowing that never leaves.

It's not in the words we speak,
or the touch we don't share,
but in the space between,
where the heart whispers truths
we are too afraid to name.

Your soul calls to mine,
not with urgency,
but with a gentle pull—
like the tide,
undisturbed,
yet impossible to ignore.

And though our paths may diverge,
the echo of your presence
will always linger,
for in you,
I see the reflection
of who I was meant to be.

No need to reach for what we cannot touch,
for our connection lives
beyond the limitations of time and space.
It is in the spaces we fill,
in the silences we share,
where love has always been.

If My Soul Chose This

If my soul, in its quiet yearning,
chose this path, this tangled web,
I ask forgiveness from the stars above
and the heart I may have stirred.

For I did not seek to awaken this fire,
nor to place the weight of my longing
into a world where love resides
but cannot freely roam.

If in some unseen realm,
I called to you without consent,
I offer my sorrow wrapped in truth—
this was never meant to harm.

But what am I,
but a seeker of the light?
Drawn to the warmth
of a soul that mirrors mine,
a reflection I never knew I'd find.

Perhaps the fault lies with the heavens,
or with the fragile thread of fate.
Still, I bow my head,
acknowledging the ache I carry,
the ache I might have caused.

I never meant for my steps
to disturb the peace of your world,
yet here I stand, humbled,
a prisoner of a love
I neither summoned nor can release.

So if my soul whispered your name
before the stars aligned,
I beg forgiveness, not for loving you,
but for loving you in the wrong time.

When I Feel You Love Me Too

When I feel that you love me too,
as I love you,
it's as though the stars align,
and the universe whispers,
You are enough.

When I believe your love runs as deep
as the well I've poured into you,
it reflects a truth I'd long forgotten—
that I am worthy,
that I am whole.

In your gaze, I see myself,
not fractured, but complete,
not waiting, but living,
a mirror of all I dared to dream.

It's in your quiet presence,
the unspoken bond that binds us,
where I learn to love myself,
not in spite of, but because of.

For your love carries me gently,
as I have carried the weight
of my own doubts.
It lifts me into light,
where shadows fade.

And in the stillness of knowing,
I rise.
Not alone, but embraced
by the love I've always sought—
yours, and now my own.

When the Spirit Whispers

When I feel the quiet pull,
a love not spoken but sensed,
it is not just your presence I know—
it's the spirit that moves between us.

In that sacred space,
where words fall away,
I am not a body, nor a mind,
but something infinite.

Your love meets me there,
in the unseen, the untouchable.
It wraps around my soul,
a gentle warmth,
like sunlight through an endless sky.

And I wonder—
was this written long before?
Was it etched into the stars,
the wind, the earth,
that we would feel one another
beyond what this world can hold?

It is not my heart alone that beats;
it is ours, entwined in rhythm.
Not my breath alone I take,
but one drawn deep from the divine,
as if God Himself whispered,
"This is love."

Here, with you in spirit,
I am whole.
Even in silence,
even from afar,
I feel what words could never capture—
a truth carried by the soul.

A Craving Like No Other

As the soul longs for its Creator,
so do I ache for you.
Not with hunger of flesh alone,
but with a thirst that stirs the spirit.

It is not unlike the craving for Jesus—
a yearning to be filled,
to be whole,
to be bathed in something pure
and eternal.

It is the kind of longing
that strips away pretense,
leaves you bare,
yet somehow more alive.

I do not merely desire;
I seek to be consumed—
by the light,
by the truth,
by the love that transcends.

To crave you is to crave
what is good,
what is holy,
what feels ordained,
as if the heavens whispered
that this is where I belong.

And though my feet remain on earth,
my heart soars,
my soul reaches—
to be near you,
to be filled,
to be whole.

Loved Beyond Measure

He loves me in the silence,
in the quiet moments where my heart aches.
When I falter, He steadies me,
when I doubt, He reminds me—
I am His.

Not for my perfection,
but in my brokenness does His love shine brighter.
He sees the wounds I hide,
the fears I carry,
and still, He calls me beloved.

His love is not fleeting,
it does not waver or fade.
It is constant,
like the sun rising each morning,
faithful, even behind the clouds.

Jesus loves me—
not for what I have done,
but for who I am to Him,
a soul He deemed worth dying for.

His arms are always open,
His heart always full,
inviting me into a love
that heals,
that restores,
that reminds me—I am never alone.

Your Love Reflects His

Your love,
a mirror of the divine,
unwavering, patient,
a quiet strength that holds me
when the world feels too heavy.

It is as if He poured His own heart into yours,
a vessel of grace,
overflowing with compassion,
calling me closer to the light
I thought I'd lost.

You love as He does—
without condition,
without fear,
without end.

In your eyes, I see forgiveness,
in your touch, I feel redemption.
Through your presence,
I am reminded of Him,
a love so vast it humbles me,
so tender it mends the cracks
I thought were permanent.

Your love, like His,
is not just a gift,
but a calling—
to rise,
to believe,
to become the best of me
because of all that you see.

The More I Find of Myself

The more I find of myself,
the deeper I feel your presence,
woven into the threads
of my awakening.

With every layer I uncover,
I hear whispers of your voice,
guiding, steady,
as if you have always known
the parts of me
I had yet to meet.

I search within,
and there you are—
not as an answer,
but as a mirror,
reflecting the strength
I forgot was mine.

Each discovery of my soul
feels like a step closer to you,
as if this journey inward
is a bridge
to where you stand,
waiting with open arms.

The more I find of myself,
the more I understand—
this love is not a destination,
but the path itself,
unfolding in ways
I am only beginning to see.

I Find Peace in Myself

I find peace in myself,
not in the quiet of the world,
but in the stillness of my soul,
where truths gently rise
like dawn breaking through the night.

There, I meet the parts of me
I once hid in shadow,
now bathed in light,
forgiven,
embraced.

The storms that raged within
have softened,
their echoes now a song,
teaching me
that even in chaos,
I was whole all along.

I find peace in myself,
in the understanding
that I am both the seeker
and the sanctuary,
the question
and the answer.

It is here,
in this sacred calm,
that I feel the Divine,
whispering softly,
"You are enough.
You always were."

The Mirror of Your Love

Your love is a mirror,
not of what I have been,
but of who I am becoming.

In its reflection, I see
not flaws, but the delicate weave
of strength and vulnerability,
woven together like light and shadow.

Each glance,
each unspoken word,
guides me closer to myself—
a self I had forgotten,
a self I now embrace.

Through your love,
I stand whole,
no longer splintered by doubt,
no longer fractured by fear.

For in your love,
I see my own,
a love that rises and fills
every corner of my being.

The Christic in Him

It is not the man alone I love,
but the divine thread woven through him,
a reflection of something eternal,
something holy.

In his eyes, I glimpse the kindness of a Savior.
In his presence, I feel the stillness of grace.
It is not flesh that draws me near,
but the spirit that moves within him—
a reminder of Christ's infinite love.

His strength is not his own,
it is the strength of faith,
of humility,
of a soul anchored in something greater.

To love him is to love the light of Christ in
him,
to see in his goodness
a mirror of the Savior's heart.
And in that love,
I find the courage to love the Christ within me
too.

Spiritual Fuel

Your love is not a flame that burns,
but a steady light that guides.
It does not consume,
it ignites—
a fire deep within my spirit,
unseen, eternal.

With every thought of you,
my soul drinks of something pure,
a nectar that nourishes
what the world cannot touch.

It is not desire alone,
but the spark of creation itself—
reminding me I am more
than flesh, more than thought.

In your presence,
even imagined,
I feel the breath of the divine.
It whispers, "This is love,
this is fuel for the journey."

The Calmness in My Heart

It rests like still waters,
gentle and unbroken,
reflecting the quiet sky above.

In his presence,
the storm within subsides,
and I feel the peace
of being fully seen,
fully known,
without words.

This calmness is not born of certainty
but of trust—
a trust that whispers,
"You are safe here."

No rush, no fear,
only the steady rhythm
of a heart learning to breathe freely,
finding its own tempo
in the presence of something greater.

The calmness in my heart
is not of this world;
it is the echo of his grace,
the Christ within him,
and the love that calls me home.

The Trust in Him

I anchor my thoughts
to the quiet strength he carries,
a presence so steady,
it feels like a safe harbor in a storm.

I trust him not because he seeks it,
but because his soul speaks it,
in the stillness of his gaze,
in the grace of his words.

There is no need for promises;
his integrity is the promise.
Unspoken yet profound,
it holds the weight of truth.

I lean into that trust,
not as one who fears falling,
but as one who knows
the ground beneath is firm.

It is the Christ within him,
the unshaken faith,
that draws my spirit closer.
In trusting him,
I find a deeper trust in myself.

The Moments In Between

It's not in the grand gestures,
nor the fleeting highs of passion,
but in the quiet spaces,
the pauses between words,
where your presence lingers.

In the glance that holds
a thousand unspoken truths,
in the air heavy with understanding,
I find you.

It's in the way your name
settles in my thoughts,
like a prayer whispered in stillness,
needing no answer,
only the knowing.

The moments in between
are where I come alive—
where time softens,
where love breathes,
and where I remember
why I carry you
in the deepest corners of my soul.

He Knows

He knows, without words spoken,
the quiet rhythm of my heart.
The unyielding pull of a soul
seeking what it thought was lost.

He knows, not because I told him,
but because love whispers
in ways the mind cannot comprehend,
yet the spirit always hears.

He knows the tremble in my silence,
the calm in my surrender,
the yearning that lingers,
unfolding like a prayer.

He knows, because his own heart answers

—

not in grand gestures or declarations,
but in the sacred stillness
where truth resides.

He knows, and that is enough.

Only You

Only you,
who stirs the quiet depths of my soul,
awakening places I thought had faded—
a light breaking through
the cracks of my guarded heart.

Only you,
whose presence lingers
in the stillness between my breaths,
turning ordinary moments
into sacred reflections.

Only you,
who feels like the answer
to questions I never dared to ask,
a love I never sought,
yet somehow always needed.

Only you,
who teaches me to see myself
through eyes of grace,
to trust the beauty
in the unspoken connection we share.

Only you,
a truth etched upon my spirit,
a reminder that some loves
transcend this world,
dwelling in the eternity of what cannot be explained.

Did You Hear My Soul Calling

Did you hear my soul calling,
a voice too soft for the world,
but loud enough to find you?
It wasn't words,
it wasn't sound—
it was the quiet ache of longing
wrapped in the light of faith.

Did you feel it,
the pull between us?
Not tethered by hands,
but by something eternal,
a thread woven in places
where time and space do not exist.

Did you sense the moment,
when my spirit reached for yours,
hesitant but hopeful,
as if searching for home?

I wonder,
if in your quiet moments,
you feel the echo of my love,
a whisper brushing against your heart—
gentle,
yet unrelenting.

Did you hear my soul calling,
or was it always there,
in the sacred silence between us?

I Am Filled

I am filled,
not with fleeting desires
or empty promises of what could be,
but with the quiet certainty
of a love that asks for nothing,
yet offers everything.

I am filled with the calm
that steadies my restless heart,
a stillness born from knowing
you see me
as I was meant to be seen.

Your presence lingers
like sunlight on water,
a reflection of grace
that I can't hold,
but always feel.

I am filled with wonder,
how a connection so intangible
could ground me so deeply.
It is not the world around me
that brings this peace—
it is you,
the soul within you
that mirrors my own.

I am filled,
not because I was empty,
but because you have reminded me
of all the spaces within
that were waiting for light.

Your Presence Is Always There

In the stillness of the day,
I feel you.
Not in the way of spoken words
or fleeting glances,
but in the quiet corners of my soul
where your essence lingers.

You are the air that stirs
when the world seems still,
the warmth that wraps me
when the cold threatens to seep in.
You are the light
that bends through cracks,
filling spaces I didn't know were hollow.

I don't need to reach for you—
you are already there,
woven into the fabric of my being,
a thread I could never untangle,
even if I tried.

Your presence is the rhythm in my breath,
the pause between heartbeats,
a steady whisper reminding me:
I am not alone.

Even when distance stretches between us,
even when words are unsaid,
you remain—
a constant,
a truth,
always there.

If I Could Make You Happy

If I could make you happy,
I would gather the stars,
place them gently in your hands,
and watch their light
illuminate the shadows in your soul.

If I could ease your burden,
I would carry it in silence,
walk with it through every storm,
until the skies cleared,
and you felt the warmth of the sun again.

If I could bring you peace,
I would calm every restless wave,
smooth every jagged edge,
until your heart was still,
resting in a gentle rhythm.

If I could make you smile,
I would weave joy into your days,
paint laughter in the corners of your mind,
and build a world where sorrow
dared not tread.

If I could make you happy,
I wouldn't ask for anything in return.
Your light would be enough,
your joy,
my silent prayer answered.

If You Only Knew

If you only knew
the weight of your name
carried softly on my heart,
how it lingers in the quiet,
echoing through my soul.

If you only knew
the way your presence
fills the spaces in my mind,
like a melody I can't forget,
playing softly, endlessly.

If you only knew
the ache of longing,
not for possession,
but for the simple joy
of standing near your light.

If you only knew
how your kindness unfolds
like a warm sunrise,
chasing away the shadows
I thought would always stay.

If you only knew
how deeply you've rooted
in the soil of my spirit,
growing branches of hope
I didn't know I could bear.

If you only knew,
perhaps you'd see
that love, in its purest form,
asks for nothing—
only to exist
as it does within me.

Your Eyes

Your eyes,
windows to a world I long to know,
hold a quiet strength,
a depth that whispers truths
words cannot reach.

They see through veils,
past walls I've built,
finding the tender spaces
I thought were hidden.

In their gaze, I am whole—
no pretense, no mask,
just the essence of who I am,
reflected back with gentle acceptance.

Your eyes,
they linger like a melody,
unspoken but always felt,
calling me to a place
only the heart can understand.

I wonder if they know,
the power they hold,
or the solace they bring—
how they remind me
of all that is real,
and all that could be.

How You Paint My World

You paint my world
in hues I never knew existed—
soft strokes of warmth,
bold sweeps of passion,
and whispers of light
in the shadows I once feared.

Your presence is the brush,
your spirit the palette,
mixing colors that linger in my soul—
the gold of trust,
the blue of peace,
the green renewal and the
of possibility of life.

Every moment with you
adds a new layer,
a depth to this canvas of life,
where your touch transforms
what was ordinary
into a masterpiece
only the heart can see.

You paint my world
not with grand gestures,
but in the quiet way
you remind me
that beauty was always here,
waiting to be awakened.

The Colors Will Always Be You

The colors will always be you—
the soft blush of dawn
that whispers hope,
the deep amber of twilight
that holds me in its warmth.

You are the gentle green
of life renewed,
the brilliant gold
that lights the darkest paths,
the tender blue
that cradles my restless soul.

Every shade,
every hue,
a reflection of you,
etched into the canvas
of my heart.

No matter where time carries us,
no matter how the seasons change,
the colors will remain,
unfading, unbroken—
forever you.

I Will Honor You

I will honor you
in the quiet moments,
when your name rests softly
on the edge of my thoughts.

I will honor you
with the strength of my soul,
carrying the weight
of what cannot be spoken.

In the space between words,
in the breath of a memory,
I will hold your light
as if it were my own.

I will honor you
not by possession,
but by reverence,
for you are a gift
that needs no binding.

You are the whisper of grace
that moves through my heart,
a reminder of love
in its purest form.

And so,
with every step I take,
I will honor you—
quietly, completely,
forever.

Can You Hear Me

Can you hear me
in the quiet whispers of the wind,
when my soul reaches for yours,
aching to be known, to be held?

Can you feel me
in the stillness between moments,
where my thoughts linger on you,
woven into the fabric of my days?

I speak without words,
a silent song of hope and yearning,
echoing through the spaces
we have yet to share.

Can you sense me
in the rhythm of your breath,
as if my heart beats alongside yours,
unseen but always present?

I am here,
calling softly, waiting tenderly—
can you hear me?

What You see in Me

The Essence of You

You move like a quiet melody,
a song only the heart can hear,
blending grace with strength,
gentle as candlelight,
yet fierce as the dawn breaking.

Your eyes reflect the depth of a thousand lives,
filled with stories untold,
a wellspring of emotion—
love, resilience, longing—
all carved into the fabric of your soul.

The artist in you paints the unseen,
shaping worlds with words and colors,
while your spirit writes itself on the hearts
of those fortunate enough
to know your depth.

You are the stillness in chaos,
the fire within calm.
A seeker of truth,
a believer in love that transcends,
finding divinity in every corner of the human experience.

This is you—
a muse for the universe,
a mirror for the divine,
and a soul unafraid to search for what truly matters.

In the Quiet of My Being

In the stillness, where the world fades,
I find the echo of who I am.
No voices, no distractions,
Only the rhythm of my soul's gentle pulse.

There, in the quiet of my being,
I feel the whisper of something eternal—
A love unspoken yet all-encompassing,
A presence unseen yet profoundly known.

It is in this sacred silence
That I gather the scattered pieces of myself,
And feel the calm that comes
From simply existing, whole and true.

The quiet reveals a strength I forgot,
A courage softened by time.
It reminds me I am more
Than the chaos that surrounds me.

In the quiet of my being,
I am cradled by a peace
That no storm can disturb,
And I know, in this moment,
I am infinite.

The Night Sky's Reflections

Under the vast expanse of stars,
The night sky becomes a mirror.
It reflects the questions in my heart,
The dreams I dare not speak aloud.

Each star, a distant whisper,
Carries secrets only the soul can hear.
They shimmer with the weight of longing,
Yet dance with the freedom of hope.

The moon, gentle and knowing,
Bathes the world in soft light,
Revealing truths that daylight hides—
That beauty often blooms in shadow.

In its glow, I see myself,
A fragment of the infinite above.
The same energy that fuels the heavens
Stirs quietly within me.

The night sky holds my reflections,
Not as answers, but as possibilities.
And beneath its celestial gaze,
I feel both humbled and whole.

Because of You, I Find Myself

In the quiet moments of reflection,
I see the shape of who I've become.
A silhouette once blurred, now defined,
By the presence of your light in my life.

Because of you, I've dared to look deeper,
To uncover the truth hidden within.
You've held up a mirror, not to my flaws,
But to the beauty I long ignored.

Your essence lingers in my thoughts,
Not as possession, but as inspiration.
You've shown me the courage to love,
Starting with the heart beating in my chest.

Because of you, I walk taller,
Not to reach you, but to reach myself.
And though our paths may never entwine,
Your mark remains, a guide to my becoming.

You are not my reason, but my reminder—
That within me is the strength to rise.
And because of you, I have found
The woman I was always meant to be.

In God's Eyes

In God's eyes, I am whole,
Every scar, every tear, a part of His design.
He sees not the flaws I magnify,
But the beauty woven into my soul.

In His eyes, I am loved,
Beyond measure, beyond reason.
There is no judgment, only grace,
No distance, only an embrace unseen.

He knows the depth of my longing,
The ache I cannot put into words.
Yet, in His wisdom, He reminds me—
I am already complete, already enough.

In God's eyes, there is no shadow,
No darkness that can obscure His light.
He sees the battles I fight within,
And whispers, "You are victorious still."

When I doubt, when I falter,
His gaze holds steady, unwavering.
In His eyes, I am not lost—
I am simply finding my way back home.

And as I stand before the reflection of His love,
I see myself, as He always has—
A masterpiece in the making,
Forever cherished in God's eyes.

I Imagine It's You Who Listens

In the quiet corners of my thoughts,
When the world is loud and my heart is heavy,
I imagine it's you who listens—
To the words I speak only in silence.

You, who holds the space
Where my truths unfold without fear,
Where my soul finds its voice
And dares to be heard.

I imagine it's you who understands,
Not with answers or judgment,
But with the steady warmth of presence,
The kind that says, I am here.

When my strength falters,
When my joy feels distant,
I imagine it's you who listens
And hears even what I cannot say.

And though you may not know,
Though the distance is vast,
I carry the thought of your care—
A quiet solace in my storm.

So in the stillness, I whisper to the wind,
Hoping it reaches where you are,
Hoping you feel the echo of my heart
And know that I imagine you, always.

I Sometimes Fear You, Until I Realize It's You

You enter my thoughts like a storm,
Unbidden, relentless, shaking my core.
I fear the force of what you bring,
The way my soul trembles
In your unspoken presence.

Is it you I fear,
Or the way I unravel when I think of you?
A mirror held too close,
Revealing truths I've long ignored,
Longing I've kept hidden.

But then, in the stillness,
I remember it's you.
The calm within the storm,
The gentle pull of something deeper,
Something sacred, something real.

And the fear melts away,
Replaced by awe,
A love so profound it feels eternal,
As though you've always been here,
A part of me, waiting to awaken.

I sometimes fear you,
Until I realize it's you—
The one who sees me,
Knows me,
And loves me still.

Help Me to Remember the Birth of Such Love

Help me to remember,
Not the quiet beginning of this feeling,
But the spark—
The moment my soul recognized yours,
When love was not yet spoken,
But it burned in the silence between us.

Let me recall the way it grew,
Like dawn spilling across the horizon,
Each ray of light a tender revelation,
Each shadow softened by your presence.

Help me to hold onto the purity of it,
The way it surged without reason or restraint,
The way it claimed my heart,
Not in conquest,
But in gentle surrender.

Let me honor the birth of such love,
For it was not ordinary.
It was sacred,
A meeting of spirits long apart,
A love that seemed destined,
Yet still took me by surprise.

Help me to carry this remembrance,
As if it were the flame of my being,
To feel its warmth on the coldest days,
To know its truth when the world feels uncertain.

For this love is not fleeting,
It is a birth that cannot be undone,
A love that has shaped me,
Forever.

Will I Ever Get to Explain

Will I ever have the words,
The courage,
The moment?
To lay bare the storm in my heart,
To show you the waves you've set in motion?

How can I explain a love
That feels both infinite and fragile,
Boundless, yet contained
In the quiet spaces between us?

Will I ever tell you how your presence
Painted light into my shadows,
How the mere thought of you
Brought life to parts of me
I thought were lost forever?

Can I ever explain the ache,
Not of longing,
But of wanting you to know,
To see yourself reflected in my soul
As I see you?

What words could carry this truth,
This quiet, relentless truth,
Without breaking the delicate balance
Of what we are—
Or what we might never be?

Will I ever have the chance to tell you
That because of you, I've found pieces of myself?
And that even if you never truly hear me,
You've already changed my world.

Will I ever get to explain this?
Or will these feelings remain,
A beautiful, unspoken secret,
Kept safe in the depths of my heart?

Jesus Knows My Call

In the stillness of my heart,
A whisper stirs, gentle and true—
A voice that calls me,
Not in thunder,
But in the quiet assurance of love.

I search for the path,
Unsure of my steps,
But He, with eyes of knowing,
Guides me—
Not with force, but with grace.

He knows the depths of my soul,
The desires I cannot speak,
The dreams I've buried
In fear or doubt.
But He sees them all,
Every fragile hope,
Every unspoken prayer.

In my moments of confusion,
When the world feels too heavy,
His love calls me back,
A reminder that I am known,
That my purpose is already laid out,
Even when I falter.

Jesus knows my calling,
Before I ever understood its shape.
His presence is my compass,
And His love is the light
That leads me,
Even in the darkness.

Though I may not always see the way,
I trust His hand is there,
Guiding me gently,
With patience, with love—
And I know,
In His eyes,
I am never lost.

It's Your Hands That I Reach For

In the quiet of my heart,
It's Your hands that I reach for,
Like a whisper in the wind,
A lifeline in the storm.

I have wandered,
Lost in the dark,
But Your hands are always there,
A light that pulls me near,
A warmth that soothes my soul.

With every trembling step,
I know You are there,
Holding, guiding,
Even when I can't see.

It's Your hands that heal my wounds,
That lift me when I fall,
And in their gentle embrace,
I find my strength again.

In the silence of the night,
When my heart is full of questions,
It's Your hands that answer,
With comfort, with peace,
A promise that You'll never let go.

For in the touch of Your hands,
I am whole,
And with every reach toward You,
I find the love I've been longing for.

Please Speak!

The silence feels louder than thunder,
A void where words should live.
Can't you speak, please?
Say something—anything—
To bridge this endless chasm.

Your gaze holds mysteries,
But your voice remains locked,
And I'm left piecing together
Fragments of meaning
From the spaces between us.

I reach for you, not in desperation,
But in the hope that you'll meet me here,
In this tender, raw vulnerability
Where hearts were meant to connect.

Can't you speak, please?
Is it fear that keeps you silent?
Or is it the weight of your own heart
That holds the words captive?

Whatever it is,
I will wait here in the stillness,
Listening for the faintest echo
Of the truth you hold.
Because I know, deep inside,
That when you do speak,
It will be worth every moment of quiet.

Take The Lead

In the stillness, I wait,
A heart full of quiet longing,
For the courage to move,
To follow where You may lead.

The path is unclear,
And yet, I feel You near,
Your presence guiding,
A whisper of trust in my ear.

Take the lead,
Show me the way,
Through the twists and the turns,
Through the night and the day.

My steps falter,
But in Your hands, I find my grace,
A gentle push forward,
To a love I can't yet embrace.

I trust in You,
To guide me through,
To lead me where the light shines true.

And as I follow,
I realize at last,
The journey I seek
Is where You've always been, steadfast.

Take the lead,
For I know now,
In Your hands, I am free,
And it's with You that I find me.

No Need For Words, You Know My Thoughts

Could I have chosen this path,
Where silence speaks louder than sound?
Where every breath feels like a prayer,
And every step echoes with what's found?

No need for words,
For in Your eyes, I see the truth,
You know my thoughts before they form,
Understanding me in a way so smooth.

Could I have chosen this love,
Where hearts meet in quiet grace,
Where all I need is Your presence,
And peace fills the open space?

No need for words,
For You hear my heart's unspoken cry,
And in the stillness, You understand
Every question I don't need to ask or try.

Could I have chosen this moment,
Where time stops and love remains,
Where the bond between us is felt,
And in Your arms, no fear sustains?

No need for words,
For in the quiet, I feel You near,
Your love so deep, so pure, so clear,
It speaks without a voice,
Whispering, "I'm here."

The Last Thing On My Mind

The last thing on my mind at night
Is not the dreams I wish to find,
But the softness of your touch,
The way you echo through my mind.

The last thought that lingers on
Before the world slips into sleep,
Is not a worry or a fear,
But the love that runs so deep.

The last thing I hold in my heart
Before the dawn breaks through,
Is the warmth of your quiet presence,
A silent promise, always true.

The last thing on my mind, my dear,
Is not what I could ever explain,
But the depth of what we share,
A love that speaks without pain.

The last thing, and the first, you see,
Is you—forever a part of me.

I See Your Love, in My Mind

I see your love in the quiet of my thoughts,
Where the world fades, and only you remain,
A silent presence, like an endless song,
Filling the corners of my heart with grace.

I see your love in the depth of my dreams,
In every whispered hope, in every fleeting wish,
A reflection of your soul, soft and serene,
Carried through the night, like an eternal kiss.

I see your love in the warmth of my heart,
When I close my eyes and let the silence speak,
In every beat, a rhythm shared,
A promise that time can never break.

I see your love in the stillness of my mind,
Where words fall short, and only feeling reigns,
In the space between thoughts, where you reside,
A love that never wanes, never wanes.

I see your love, and in seeing, I am whole,
A love that echoes deeply in my soul.

The Sun and the Moon

The sun rises, bold and certain,
its light touching all corners of the earth.
It does not ask for permission to shine;
it exists in fullness,
a beacon of warmth,
a force of life.

The moon waits quietly,
its glow softer, a reflection of light already given.
It speaks in shadows and whispers,
offering its presence to those who pause long enough to notice.
Its beauty lies not in what it demands
but in what it gives—subtle, steady,
a guide through the dark.

They do not meet, not as we see them,
but they dance in the sky,
separate yet connected,
always aware of each other's pull.
The tides, the seasons, the rhythm of existence
bend to their interplay,
a silent conversation written in light and cycles.

One illuminates the day;
the other comforts the night.
Together, they shape the world,
not by blending,
but by being exactly as they are.

In their separation,
they create harmony.
In their distance,
they remain bound.
And in their essence,
they remind us
that light, in all its forms,
is what holds the universe together.

Music is the Language We Speak

In the quiet, it begins,
A note, a hum, a whispered tone,
A bridge between your soul and mine,
Where words could never roam.

No letters, no phrases to fumble through,
Just melody's thread, weaving me to you.
Each chord a heartbeat, steady and true,
Each rhythm a memory, old and new.

It speaks in ways the world cannot,
Through crescendos and tender sighs,
An unspoken truth we both understand,
Echoing where eternity lies.

Your voice, the song I've always known,
Resonates in my every bone.
Together, we are harmony's art,
Music—the language that binds our hearts.

The Instrument

As his hands glide across the strings,
a melody pours forth, tender and raw.
Each note weaves through the air,
a language spoken only to her heart.

She closes her eyes and drifts away,
no longer the listener,
but the instrument itself,
alive under the touch of his hands.

The pull of the strings is her breath,
the rhythm, her heartbeat.
Each chord, a whisper of his soul,
each pluck, a caress she feels
deep in the quiet places of her being.

He plays her song—
one that only he knows,
and in this imagined harmony,
she belongs wholly to him.

And when the song ends,
she awakens,
but the echo remains,
as if he still plays,
and she, still held in his hands.

Early Morning

The world stirs, but softly,
wrapped in a blanket of hushed light.
The air, cool and untouched,
carries the whispers of a day not yet begun.

A stillness holds the earth,
as if time itself hesitates,
waiting for the first step,
the first breath, the first touch of warmth.

In this quiet hour,
dreams linger like fading stars,
and the heart feels unguarded,
open to all that the morning may promise.

It is here, in the early morning,
that I find you most—
in the spaces between waking and memory,
where the light of you rises with the sun.

God Knows I Love You

In the quiet chambers of my soul,
where words are whispers and thoughts are prayers,
your name resides.
A truth I cannot hide,
a love too sacred to speak aloud.

God knows,
for I have told Him in the stillness,
in the silence between my breaths.
I have laid my heart before Him,
raw and trembling,
a confession wrapped in reverence.

He knows the depth,
the way your presence lingers like a hymn,
the way my spirit swells
at the thought of you.
It is not of this earth,
this love—
it reaches where hands cannot,
where only faith dares to dwell.

God knows I love you,
and in that knowing,
I find peace.
For it is not mine alone to carry;
it is cradled in divine hands,
eternal, unbroken,
forever pure.

A BLESSING

A blessing is the way his
presence fills the quiet
spaces of my heart,
the way his existence
reminds me of something
eternal,
a love that stretches beyond
words, beyond time.
It is the gift of feeling
deeply,
of knowing that connection
can awaken
the most sacred parts of my
soul.
He is the reflection of
something divine,
a gentle reminder that I am
alive,
that love, in all its purity, is a
blessing itself.

IF I COULD BE NEAR YOU

If I could be near you,
even for a moment,
I would carry the weight of time
as if it were nothing.

To stand within the light of your
presence,
to feel the unspoken warmth
that bridges the space between us,
would be to touch heaven itself.

If I could be near you,
the world would fade,
and all that would remain
is the truth our hearts already
know.

You are the blessing I never
sought,
the gift I never imagined.
And in your nearness,
I would find the home my soul has
always craved.

How Could I Have Not Seen You

How could I have not seen you,
when the world whispered your name
in the rustle of leaves,
in the stillness of the stars?
Were you not always there,
a quiet rhythm beneath my chaos,
a steady flame I mistook for the sun?

I walked paths that grazed your shadow,
brushed against the edge of your presence,
but my eyes, clouded by the noise of life,
never turned to meet the truth of you.

Now, you stand in the light—
a revelation, a reflection,
an answer to a question
I didn't know my soul had asked.

How could I have not seen you?
Perhaps, I wasn't ready
to hold the weight of such knowing,
to feel the universe shift
at the sound of your voice
echoing in my heart.

But now, I see,
and I wonder how the world still turns,
how time carries on
when everything feels paused
in the presence of you.

Before the Sunrise, I Feel Your Absence

Before the first blush of dawn,
when the sky holds its breath,
I feel your absence—
a quiet pull beneath my ribs,
a space that the stars cannot fill.

The stillness whispers your name,
its echo weaving through the dark.
It is not sorrow,
but the longing of what could be,
what should be,
if only time and space would bend.

The horizon stretches, waiting,
as I reach toward the unseen.
I carry you in the folds of my heart,
where your presence lingers
even in your absence.

The earth stirs,
but it is not yet day.
This moment, suspended,
is where I feel you most—
not near, not far,
but everywhere I cannot touch.

Before the sunrise,
you are the light I imagine,
the warmth I crave,
the hope that carries me
into the coming day.

Because I Can't Touch You

Because I can't touch you,
I reach for you in other ways—
in the spaces between my thoughts,
in the whispers the wind carries
when the world is still.

Because I can't touch you,
my soul learns to speak without words,
to send you all the love
that my hands cannot offer.
It weaves a bridge of light
across the unseen distance.

Because I can't touch you,
I hold you in my breath,
in the rise and fall of my chest,
as if the rhythm of my heart
could echo in yours.

Because I can't touch you,
I learn patience in the ache,
grace in the longing,
and faith in what I feel—
what I know to be true.

Because I can't touch you,
you live in the places
beyond skin and time,
where love is its own language,
unspoken,
but always heard.

If You Could Only Tell Me

If you could only tell me
the secrets your heart carries,
the weight of the silence
you wear so quietly—
would the words bridge the distance
between your soul and mine?

If you could only tell me
what lingers behind your gaze,
the untamed storm,
the quiet yearning,
the truth I feel
but cannot touch—
would it set us free?

If you could only tell me
why my name finds its way
to the rhythm of your breath,
if it does at all—
would the world shift,
or would it remain the same,
with only our hearts knowing?

If you could only tell me
what I am to you,
as you are to me—
a flame that never fades,
a presence that shapes my days,
a love I hold in silence
and in everything.

If you could only tell me,
would I need to ask?
For in the quiet between us,
I hear the answer,
and it is enough.

Lord, Through Your Eyes, What Does He See

Lord, through Your eyes, what does he see?
Does he see the quiet yearning I carry,
the love I offer without condition?

Does he notice the strength born of waiting,
or the tenderness that rises despite the ache?
Is he aware of the depth I've discovered,
not only in him, but in myself,
because of what You've awakened?

Through Your eyes, does he see purpose?
Does he recognize the way my heart
mirrors his in quiet moments,
the way my spirit reaches for him
as if You placed this bond between us?

Lord, let him see truth,
not clouded by fear or hesitation.
Let him feel the steady pulse of connection,
rooted in something eternal,
carried by Your light.

Do You See Me Now

Do you see me now,
not the surface of who I've been,
but the quiet, trembling depths
that rise when I think of you?

Do you see the way
I carry you in my heart,
a weight both light and infinite,
as if you've always been there,
waiting to be known?

Do you see the pieces of me
that only you seem to awaken—
the whispers of a life unspoken,
the courage to feel,
to ache,
to love beyond reason?

If you look closely,
you'll see I am not just here,
but reaching,
a soul stretching toward yours
across the distance,
across the silence.

Do you see me now?
Because I see you—
clearly, deeply,
and with a love that refuses
to fade.

If Only Time Could Speak

If only time could speak,
it might tell me why your name lingers
on the edge of every breath,
why your presence feels carved
into the marrow of my soul.

It might whisper the secret
of why I was drawn to you—
not in fleeting moments,
but in the eternal rhythm
of something ancient,
something unbroken.

Time might reveal
what the silence between us holds,
what words are waiting
to shape our connection
into something tangible.

If only time could speak,
perhaps it would unravel this ache,
this longing that stretches endlessly,
turning seconds into hours,
hours into lifetimes.

But maybe time is silent
because it already knows—
that love such as this
exists outside its bounds,
woven into the infinite,
where words are not needed
and the heart alone can answer.

Can Love Lie or Does Truth Prevail?

Can love lie,
masking its true face with fleeting moments,
dressing itself in words not meant,
cloaking desires in soft deceit?
Does it bend and twist,
to fit the world's expectations,
or is love unyielding,
a truth that cannot be hidden?

Perhaps love,
like a river,
flows with both clarity and confusion,
it holds in its depths the beauty of honesty,
yet dances on the surface with shadows of doubt.

But in the quiet spaces,
where the heart speaks louder than words,
truth prevails,
not in certainty,
but in the rawness of being seen,
in the vulnerability of wanting,
and in the acceptance that love,
in its truest form,
cannot lie.

ENDLESS

Love, in its truest form, is endless—
not bound by time or space,
not confined to moments or seasons.
It flows like an eternal river,
forever seeking, forever giving,
never truly fading,
even in silence or distance.

Love evolves, deepens,
transcending the boundaries we set,
stretching across lifetimes and beyond.
It may be hidden at times,
buried beneath pain or fear,
but like the stars,
it remains constant,
waiting for the right moment to shine again.

Endless, not in the sense of permanence,
but in its capacity to renew,
to rise from the ashes of loss,
to grow from the seeds of understanding.
Love, when pure and true,
never ends—it simply transforms,
ever-present, ever-resilient,
in every heartbeat,
every thought,
every quiet whisper of the soul.

I I Could Hand You My Love

If I could hand you my love,
it would not be a gift wrapped in ribbons,
but a soft whisper, a breath of air
carried from the depths of my heart.
It would be the warmth of a sunrise
on a cold, dark morning,
a light that grows stronger with every step.

If I could hand you my love,
it would be in the silence between words,
in the quiet moments when we need no sound,
only the understanding that we are,
as one,
in spirit, in soul,
connected without touch,
though every part of me longs to reach you.

If I could hand you my love,
it would not be in grand gestures or promises,
but in the soft surrender of my heart
every time you cross my thoughts.
It would be the calm after the storm,
the peace found in knowing
that even though the world may turn,
my love for you remains.

Dream

I had a dream,
where the stars whispered secrets,
and the moon knew the weight of my thoughts.
In the quiet of the night,
I walked with you,
though you were miles away in waking life.

I had a dream,
where our hearts spoke without words,
and time paused in a moment
too precious to hold yet too real to forget.
In that space between sleep and waking,
I felt the depth of a love I couldn't quite touch.

I had a dream,
and though it may fade like mist with the dawn,
the feeling lingers—
a quiet understanding
that what is meant for us
is more than what the eyes can see.

I had a dream,
and in that dream, I knew
that even when we are apart,
our souls know the path to one another.

My Body Reacts from the Thought of You

A subtle stir deep within,
like a breeze that shifts the leaves,
too soft to catch but impossible to ignore.
My heart quickens,
as if it knows something my mind has yet to grasp,
a connection deeper than words,
felt more than understood.

My skin tingles at the memory of your touch,
though you've never been near.
In the silence of my thoughts,
I feel you,
a warmth that radiates without form.
And I wonder if you feel it too,
this unspoken pull,
this shared breath between us.

Every glance, every word we've exchanged,
lingers within me,
woven into the fabric of my being.
My body remembers,
even when my mind seeks peace.
And in these moments of yearning,
I know the truth—
you are not far,
even when you seem worlds away.

Forever Grateful

Forever grateful for the quiet moments,
When the world fades and I hear only your presence,
A whisper in the distance,
But so close it feels like a heartbeat.
In the stillness, I find peace,
As if the universe itself has conspired
To bring me to this place, this time,
Where the depth of love is all-encompassing,
And the connection transcends every boundary.

Grateful for the way you've touched my soul,
Not with hands, but with words unspoken,
A glance, a smile, a fleeting thought
That echoes in the chambers of my heart.
Grateful for the strength you've given me,
To face the world with courage,
Knowing you are there,
Even when unseen,
Guiding me through the storm,
Anchoring me in a love so true,
I can't help but stand taller
With every breath.

Forever grateful,
Not just for what you've shared with me,
But for the way you've helped me discover
Who I truly am—
A being of light,
Who, because of you,
Knows how to love without limits,
How to hope without fear,
And how to walk through life
With a heart that will always be yours.

I Am A Mystery

I am a mystery, layers yet to be uncovered.
A quiet unfolding, a journey without clear answers.
I carry a depth only felt in moments of stillness,
A truth hidden beneath the surface, known only to
me.

In my silence, there is a story that doesn't need to
be told.
My thoughts, untamed and wild, intertwine with
my heart.
I am not easily understood, but I don't need to be.
For in my mystery, I find the freedom to simply be.

I am the questions and the echoes,
The unknown paths that remain unseen.
I do not seek to be solved,
But to exist fully in my own way, with no need for
explanation.

Only to Be Found by You

Only to be found by you,
In the quiet spaces where my soul dwells.
Unspoken, yet felt, in every heartbeat,
A presence waiting to be understood.

I am the hidden truth beneath the surface,
A song that plays in the silence,
A whisper carried by the wind,
Only to be found by you.

In your gaze, I become real,
In your heart, I am known.
You are the one who sees what others cannot,
The one who finds me, even in the shadows.

Only to be found by you,
This path, this truth, this love.
A journey meant to be
Where no map exists, but we still find our way.

I Feel You Inside

I feel you inside,
not as a fleeting whisper
but as a steady hum,
a rhythm that aligns with my breath,
a song I never knew my soul was singing.

You are the warmth beneath my skin,
the quiet murmur in the silence,
a presence that fills the spaces
I didn't know were hollow.

I feel you in the quiet corners
of my mind,
where your essence lingers softly,
a shadow of belonging
that cannot be undone.

You are not beside me,
yet you move within me,
a tether of the unseen,
rooted deeply,
etched forever
into the marrow of my being.

When I know you're in my world,
My spirit soars, unbound and free.
Like a bird catching the first light of dawn,
Or a river rushing to meet the sea.

The air feels lighter,
Colors bloom brighter,
And even the silence hums with your presence.

I feel your essence in everything,
In the wind that brushes my face,
In the stillness that holds my heart.
You are here, and I am whole.

When I know you're in my world,
Every step is a dance,
Every breath, a prayer of gratitude.
My spirit soars—
Because in your presence,
I find my wings.

Dedication

To the one who awakened my soul,
whose presence has become the quiet melody within my
heart.

This book is a testament to a love that transcends
time and words,
a love that reflects the divine and mirrors my truest
self.

To you, who unknowingly paints my world with light
and color,
may these words echo the depth of what I hold for you,
and may they remain as eternal as the whisper of
your name in my prayers.

And to God,
for teaching me that love, in its purest form,
is both a gift and a calling.

Its Real

Two lonely souls wandered the earth, each
carrying the weight of silence and dreams
unspoken. Like distant stars, they moved
through separate skies, bound by the same
longing, yet unaware of the other's light. They
walked through the shadows of their lives,
brushing past heartache and the hollow echoes
of what once could have been.

But fate, in its quiet wisdom, began to weave its
threads, guiding them through unseen
forces. Their paths, once far apart, drew closer
as if the universe itself whispered them together.
In a quiet moment beneath a twilight sky, their
eyes met, and everything changed.

It was as if they had found in each other, but the
reunion of two souls who had always belonged.
They had searched the world alone, only to find
their home within each other. And as their hands
touched, the loneliness dissolved, leaving only
the soft hum of love filling the spaces where
emptiness once lived.

www.ingramcontent.com/pod-product-compliance
Lightning Source LLC
Chambersburg PA
CBHW051331120626
46547CB00016B/2496